SilverTip

Electric Vehicles

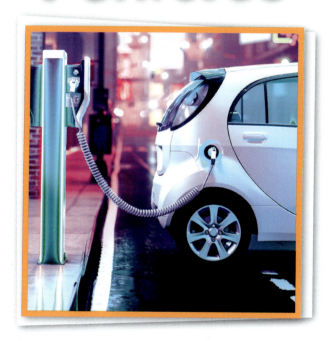

by Ashley Kuehl

Consultant: Caitlin Krieck, Social Studies Teacher and
Instructional Coach, The Lab School of Washington

BEARPORT
PUBLISHING

Minneapolis, Minnesota

T0413947

Credits

Cover and title page, © onurdongel/iStock; 5, © Brandon Woyshnis/Adobe Stock; 7, © Ariel Krysztofiak/ Adobe Stock; 8, © zayacsk/Adobe Stock; 9, © felix mizioznikov/Adobe Stock; 11, © Mike Mareen /Adobe Stock; 13, © BASILICOSTUDIO STOCK/Adobe Stock; 15, © SuperStock/Alamy Stock Photo; 16, © algre/ Shutterstock; 17, © Cynthia Lee/Alamy Stock Photo; 19, © uflypro/Adobe Stock; 21, © SV Production/ Shutterstock; 23, © milehightraveler/iStock; 25, © EZEQUIEL BECERRA/Getty Images; 27, © Laser1987/ iStock; 28TL, © Sipa USA/Alamy Stock Photo; 28ML, © Public Domain/Wikimedia; 28BL, © Newsday LLC/ Getty Images

Bearport Publishing Company Product Development Team

Publisher: Jen Jenson; Director of Product Development: Spencer Brinker; Managing Editor: Allison Juda; Editor: Cole Nelson; Associate Editor: Naomi Reich; Associate Editor: Tiana Tran; Art Director: Colin O'Dea; Designer: Kim Jones; Designer: Kayla Eggert; Product Development Specialist: Owen Hamlin

Statement on Usage of Generative Artificial Intelligence

Bearport Publishing remains committed to publishing high-quality nonfiction books. Therefore, we restrict the use of generative AI to ensure accuracy of all text and visual components pertaining to a book's subject. See BearportPublishing.com for details.

Quote Sources

Page 28: Jim Farley from "Ford CEO Jim Farley posts an insightful ode to electric vehicles as a 'lifelong petrol head'," *electrek*, June 28, 2024; Mike Crapo from "Crapo Legislation to Defund Biden's Electric Vehicle Mandate Receives Senate Vote," *Mike Crapo U.S. Senator for Idaho*, Apr. 18, 2024; Michaelle C. Solages from "Harckham, Advocates Announce New Bill to Spur Zero-Emission Vehicle Sales in New York," *The New York State Senate*, Feb. 12, 2024.

Library of Congress Cataloging-in-Publication Data

Names: Kuehl, Ashley, 1977- author.
Title: Electric vehicles / by Ashley Kuehl.
Description: Minneapolis, Minnesota : Bearport Publishing Company, [2025] |
   Series: In the news : need to know | Includes bibliographical references
   and index.
Identifiers: LCCN 2024035365 (print) | LCCN 2024035366 (ebook) | ISBN
   9798892327633 (library binding) | ISBN 9798892329415 (paperback) | ISBN
   9798892328500 (ebook)
Subjects: LCSH: Electric vehicles--Juvenile literature. | Hybrid electric
   vehicles--Juvenile literature. | Greenhouse gases--Environmental
   aspects--Juvenile literature.
Classification: LCC TL220 .K84 2025 (print) | LCC TL220 (ebook) | DDC
   629.22/93--dc23/eng/20240813
LC record available at https://lccn.loc.gov/2024035365
LC ebook record available at https://lccn.loc.gov/2024035366

For more information, write to Bearport Publishing, 5357 Penn Avenue South, Minneapolis, MN 55419.

Contents

A Smooth Ride

A quiet car zips by. Unlike others on the road, it doesn't leave behind a trail of **emissions**. How is that possible? The car doesn't use gasoline. It's an electric vehicle (EV). When it gets low, it's time to plug in rather than visit the pump.

Gasoline-fueled cars make **carbon dioxide**. This gas comes out the car's tailpipe. Carbon dioxide can hurt people and the planet. EVs do not make the harmful gas.

Burning Fuel, Harming Earth

Most cars are powered by gasoline. Their engines burn this **fossil fuel** to make energy. But burning gasoline makes **greenhouse gases**. These gases get stuck in the **atmosphere** around the planet. They make Earth hotter. This can also cause other weather problems around the world.

Gasoline comes from plants and animals that died long ago. They turn into fossil fuels over millions of years.

Many electric vehicles don't use gasoline. Most have batteries. People charge the batteries by plugging the car in, a lot like charging a phone. As the car drives, it uses electricity from the battery. When the electricity is used up, it's time to charge again.

A few electric vehicles use **hydrogen** as fuel. They mix the hydrogen with oxygen to turn it into energy. These cars need special fuel stations. But there aren't very many of these stations around yet.

Mixing It Up

Some vehicles use a mix of gasoline and electricity. A **hybrid** electric vehicle has both a battery and a gasoline engine. As the engine burns the gasoline, it charges the battery. Then, this battery can help power the car.

There are also plug-in hybrid vehicles. These cars plug into a power source to charge. When their batteries run low on power, their engines can burn gasoline to charge the batteries.

A hybrid uses less gasoline than an all-gasoline-powered car.

Just Charge It

EVs plug into electric charging stations to fill their batteries. Many people charge their vehicles at home. They plug into power from their home's electrical system.

Cities and businesses also have charging stations. Some are free to use. Others cost money.

Most home charging stations work slowly. Sometimes, it can take 40 hours to charge an EV. Public stations are often faster. But drivers may have to pay to use them.

What Do We Love?

One of the biggest reasons people like EVs is that the cars don't need gasoline. EVs don't put greenhouse gases into the air. Drivers don't have to spend their money on the fuel.

Many governments give **tax credits** to people who buy EVs. That means the buyers may pay less in taxes later.

The energy used in an EV is better for Earth than gasoline. But it's not perfect. Many power companies burn fossil fuels to make electricity. That adds greenhouse gases to the air.

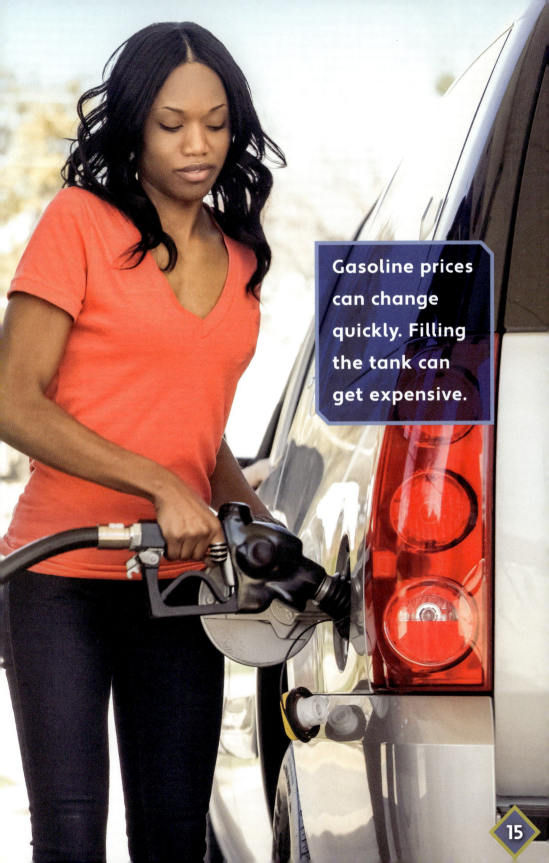

Gasoline prices can change quickly. Filling the tank can get expensive.

Gasoline-fueled cars have complex engines. There are a lot of moving parts. And they use oil and other liquids. EVs don't use these substances. The cars are cleaner.

The simpler EV engines take less work to **maintain**. EV drivers need to get work done on their cars less often.

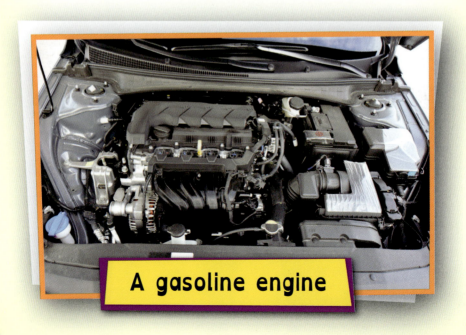

A gasoline engine

Car makers want people to buy their vehicles. They try to build EVs that are beautiful and fun to drive.

What's Not to Love?

EVs do have some problems. Most can go only short distances before they need to charge. Charging the battery can take a long time, even overnight. Fast charging stations cost more to use.

It can also be hard to find charging stations. They're less common than gas stations.

Weather can affect an EV's charge. Cold weather uses up battery power faster. During colder seasons, EVs need to be charged more often.

Another challenge with EVs is the price. EVs cost more than gasoline-fueled cars.

EV batteries are also expensive. They usually last about 10 years. But then they need to be changed. A new EV battery costs a lot more than a gasoline-powered car battery.

It takes a lot of special **minerals** to make an EV battery. Gathering these materials from the planet can harm the environment. There is also a limited amount on Earth. We may run out.

EV batteries

Limits and Laws

Even with the problems, EVs are on the rise. Part of this is because of new laws. Countries are limiting the amount of emissions new cars can make. To hit these goals, new cars will have to use less gasoline for fuel. So, there will likely be more EVs.

Some people don't want emissions laws to change. There are those who say new limits are unfair to people who can't afford EVs. Gasoline companies also want cars to keep using the fossil fuel.

Emissions can make the air around cities very dirty.

Lower Prices, Higher Numbers

Some companies are starting to make EVs that are cheaper. This will take away a big challenge for many. More people may be able to buy and drive EVs for less. As this happens, more EVs may hit the streets.

Some drivers have been making their own EVs. They change the engines of gasoline-fueled cars. This costs much less than buying a new EV.

This gasoline-powered car is being turned electric.

NEWS

Imagining the Future

Many people believe that within 10 years, half of all cars and trucks will be electric. And they won't be the only electric vehicles out there. Engineers are also working on electric boats, buses, and even planes. The future is looking electric.

California made a law to push for EVs. By 2035, all new cars there will need to make zero emissions.

Voices in the News

People have many things to say about electric vehicles. Some of their voices can be heard in the news.

Jim Farley
CEO of Ford Motor Company

"For me and for millions of Americans, electric vehicles are removing daily hassles and reminding us why we love to drive."

Mike Crapo
United States Senator

"Emissions standards go too far and will restrict affordable vehicle choices for our families."

Michaelle C. Solages
New York State Assembly Representative

"If we are to address the climate crisis, we need to take urgent action. Making it easier . . . to purchase electric vehicles is one common sense step that we should take immediately."

⭐ SilverTips for REVIEW

Review what you've learned. Use the text to help you.

Define key terms

charging
electric vehicle
emissions

greenhouse gases
hybrid

Check for understanding

What is an electric vehicle, and how is it different from a gasoline-fueled vehicle?

Name one good thing about electric vehicles.

What is one drawback of electric vehicles?

Think deeper

Do you think electric vehicles are good for our world? Why or why not?

⭐ SilverTips on TEST-TAKING

- **Make a study plan.** Ask your teacher what the test is going to cover. Then, set aside time to study a little bit every day.

- **Read all the questions carefully.** Be sure you know what is being asked.

- **Skip any questions** you don't know how to answer right away. Mark them and come back later if you have time.

Glossary

atmosphere the layer of gases that surround Earth

carbon dioxide a gas given off when fossil fuels are burned

emissions gases put in the air by fuel-burning engines

fossil fuel a fuel made from remains of animals and plants that died long ago

greenhouse gases gases in the air that trap heat around Earth

hybrid a vehicle with two power sources, usually gasoline and electricity

hydrogen a simple, lightweight gas sometimes used as fuel

maintain to keep in good condition

minerals substances found in nature that are not plants or animals

tax credits amounts of money subtracted from the taxes people owe

Read More

Bergin, Raymond. *Vehicles (X-Treme Facts: Engineering).* Minneapolis: Bearport Publishing, 2023.

Gardner, Jane Parks. *Electricity (Intro to Physics: Need to Know).* Minneapolis: Bearport Publishing, 2023.

Heitkamp, Kristina Lyn. *Electric Vehicles (Focus on Current Events).* Lake Elmo, MN: Focus Readers, 2022.

Learn More Online

1. Go to **FactSurfer.com** or scan the QR code below.

2. Enter "**Electric Vehicles**" into the search box.

3. Click on the cover of this book to see a list of websites.

Index

About the Author

Ashley Kuehl is an editor and writer specializing in nonfiction for young people. She lives in Minneapolis, MN.